GPK

Remembering Grace

Photographs by Howell Conant

Text by Kay and Digby Diehl
Designed by Rick DeMonico
A Bob Adelman Book

LIFE GREAT PHOTOGRAPHER SERIES

LIFE Books Editor **Robert Sullivan**

Bob Adelman Books Inc.
Text by **Kay and Digby Diehl**
Art Director **Rick DeMonico**
Digital Imaging **Stephen Watt**

Time Inc. Home Entertainment
Publisher **Richard Fraiman**
General Manager **Steven Sandonato**
Executive Director, Marketing Services **Carol Pittard**
Director, Retail & Special Sales **Tom Mifsud**
Director, New Product Development **Peter Harper**
Assistant Director, Brand Marketing **Laura Adam**
Assistant General Counsel **Dasha Smith Dwin**
Book Production Manager **Jonathan Polsky**
Design & Prepress Manager **Anne-Michelle Gallero**
Marketing Manager **Alexandra Bliss**

Special Thanks to:
Bozena Bannett
Glenn Buonocore
Suzanne Janso
Robert Marasco
Brooke Reger
Mary Sarro-Waite
Ilene Schreide
Adriana Tierno
Alex Voznesenskiy

Published by Time Inc. Home Entertainment Books
LIFE is a trademark of Time Inc.

Time Inc.
1271 Avenue of the Americas
New York, New York 10020

We welcome your comments and suggestions about TIHE Books. Please write to us at:
TIHE Books
Attention: Book Editors
PO Box 11016
Des Moines, IA 50336-1016

If you would like to order any of our hardcover Collector's Edition books, please call us at 1-800-327-6388.
(Monday through Friday, 7:00 a.m.– 8:00 p.m. or Saturday,
7:00 a.m.– 6:00 p.m. Central Time).

Table of Contents

Introduction

It was an extraordinary friendship between photographer and subject, and one that is unique in celebrity photography. Howell Conant's amazing eye and Grace Kelly's confidence in him created a new look in Hollywood portraits: natural glamour. Together they broke the cold stereotype of Hurrell-style goddess photos. Although Grace personally approved of every Conant photo published during her lifetime, some of the most intimate images included here have never been published before.

Over a period that spanned 27 years, from the zenith of her Hollywood fame to her tragic death in 1982, Howell captured Grace in a wide range of settings, both formal and familial. He was not only her official photographer, he was her confidant, and had unique access to Grace in her most private moments. The legacy of this singular collaboration is a time-lapse testament to the blossoming of a movie legend into a princess, and her flowering as a wife, mother, and royal role model.

Photography ran in Howell's blood. Born in Marinette, Wisconsin, his father was a portrait photographer, as were his grandfather, two uncles, and two cousins. The Conants made their living photographing milestone family events in the rural community on Sturgeon Bay. As a kid, Howell apprenticed with his father. He loved it, even though his feelings about taking portraits at endless christenings, weddings, and graduations were lukewarm at best.

Howell enlisted in the Navy the day after Pearl Harbor, and the Navy immediately put his skill behind the camera to use. He spent the war assigned to an elite photo unit attached to Admiral Chester Nimitz's staff, and rose to become its highest ranking enlisted man, riding herd on 350 photographers in the Pacific theatre. After the war he headed for New York, and in 1950 opened his own commercial studio, specializing in advertising and fashion photography.

His friendship with Grace began with a cover assignment from the movie fan magazine *Photoplay* early in 1955. At the time, she was already a Hollywood hot property, but had not yet won her Oscar for *The Country Girl*. Howell was already experienced at taking movie star glamour shots, but when he looked at the young Grace thorough his lens, he stopped. Transfixed by her beauty, he became uncharacteristically hesitant behind the camera. On a tight schedule, Grace quickly became her own art director. She curtly showed him her best camera angles and urged him to set his lights and get on with it.

There it might have ended, but for a headband. Grace's next stop was to be an interview with influential gossip columnist Earl Wilson (the Liz Smith of his day), and on the way out the door she asked to borrow a headband from Howell's inventory. He readily agreed to the loan, provided that Grace bring the item back herself. When she returned, she was drawn to some of Howell's underwater photos. A scuba enthusiast, one of his favorite subjects was the U-853, a German submarine that had been sunk in the very last days of the war, not far from his Block Island summer home.

By this time, Howell had landed another assignment to shoot Grace, this time for *Collier's*, a popular weekly variety magazine. The magazine had already tossed a number of concepts at her for the session, but she'd nixed all of them. It is possible that this may have been because the suggestions were mundane; it may also have been because Grace was exhausted. She had been working at a frenetic pace, shooting and promoting six films – *Dial M for Murder, Rear Window, Green Fire, The Bridges at Toko-Ri, The Country Girl,* and the yet-to-be released *To Catch a Thief* – in less than twelve months.

Grace was burnt out, and needed some time off. She and her sister Peggy, a frequent companion, headed to Jamaica for a vacation. Shortly after arriving, she sent for Howell. He could shoot the *Collier's* assignment while she was on holiday.

Howell Conant's iconic photo of Grace rising from the green waters of the Caribbean, hair slicked back, shoulders bare, eyes intensely blue, is still gorgeous, but in some ways that is the least impressive thing about it. Because she was unquestionably beautiful and knew how to play to the camera, it wasn't difficult to capture a lovely image of her face. For Howell, however, that was never enough. From the outset of his career, he'd wanted more.

And so did she. "I never want to dress up a picture with just my face," she declared, and consistently sought out roles with more meat on them. That steely determination put Grace squarely at odds with MGM, which in the dying days of the iron-fisted studio system had her under contract for three films a year. Underestimating her as little more than this year's blonde, studio head

The princely couple bestows a royal focusing cloth on Howell, 1957.

Dore Schary kept trying to force-feed her a steady diet of fluff parts in flyweight films.

Grace batted down these proposals as soon as they were put forward, and threatened to abandon Hollywood entirely. "If anybody starts using me as scenery," she vowed, "I'll return to New York." Her intransigence almost got her suspended at the studio, but Grace didn't blink — after all, she came from a wealthy family and didn't need the money. "All the men can duel and fight," she said about one clunker she rejected (*Quentin Durward*, a costume epic), "but all I'd do would be to wear 35 different costumes, and look frightened and pretty."

As a photographer, Howell was constantly striving for innovation, but he had nothing against beauty. A meticulous craftsman and tireless worker, he put great personal energy and enthusiasm into each session. "Getting a good photograph – that's hard work. It's no fun unless I'm out to get something different each time," he'd said.

He also believed in a very simple axiom: good photos make people look good. "It's easy to make people look bad, and say it's a character study," he said. "I always liked people to look pretty." With Grace, however, Howell repeatedly caught something more than her beautiful face, and it was this ability that initially won her favor, and thereafter her loyalty and admiration.

From the first shot in Jamaica in 1955 to his last session with her in 1981, Howell's pictures of Grace have a vitality that invites us to linger and speculate on what lies beneath. The earliest photos convey a warmth that suggests something smoldering behind that flawless patrician façade — what the Hollywood wags insisted on calling her "Ice Queen" veneer. Whatever that something was, it was not only undeniably sexy, but fresh, natural, and classy at the same time.

For Hollywood, this "natural glamour" was impressively new. In the movies, sex appeal had always been associated with bimbos, vamps, tarts, and hussies; it had vulgar overtones of sleaze. Grace Kelly wrapped it up in a Tiffany box, and invited us to tug on the ribbon. Some said she inspired "licit passion." Alfred Hitchcock, who was smitten with her, called it "sexual elegance."

The *Collier's* cover of Grace in Jamaica had that quality and then some, and it proved to be Howell's money shot. When that issue hit the newsstands, there wasn't a woman in America who didn't wish she looked that good all wet. And there wasn't a man alive who didn't want to take her home to mother.

The timing coincided with Grace's coronation as the queen of Hollywood. Her star had been on the rise since she'd replaced the psychologically troubled Gene Tierney in *Mogambo* late in 1952, but a year later she was still a second choice actress, getting roles that had first been given to others. When she was cast in *The Country Girl*, it was as a stand-in for Jennifer Jones, who had become pregnant right before the beginning of principal photography. (Because it was made at Paramount, Grace had to do battle with Schary for permission to take the part.)

Howell mugs behind Princess Grace in Switzerland, 1959.

By the time *Collier's* came out on June 24, 1955, however, Grace Kelly had catapulted far beyond anyone's idea of first runner-up. After her acclaimed performance in *Rear Window* and her Oscar night besting of Judy Garland (who, it is said, never got over it), Grace's popularity supernovaed. By June of 1955, Grace Kelly was Hollywood's go-to girl, the #1 name-above-the-title box office attraction, all at the age of 25.

By June of 1955, the die had also been cast for the rest of her life. Grace had led the U.S. delegation to the Cannes Film Festival in May, where *The Country Girl* was to be screened. After a chance encounter with a *Paris Match* reporter (who wanted nothing more than a royalty photo op – the Prince of Monaco meets the Queen of Hollywood), an introduction was arranged with Prince Rainier Monaco's bachelor head of state. There was no need for an interpreter. Grace had a decent command of schoolgirl French, but Rainier, who was raised with an English nanny and attended an exclusive British boarding school, spoke impeccable English.

After the meeting, Grace declared the prince to be "charming," but nothing further appeared to come of it. Rainier resumed being a prince. Grace wrote her thank-you note (as a well brought up young lady would do) and went back to Cannes before heading home.

Meanwhile, Howell Conant was busy beating back the crowds of would-be clients at his door. Both Hollywood and Madison Avenue were queued up, begging for his services. A bevy of Hollywood actresses, among them Elizabeth Taylor, Audrey Hepburn, Janet Leigh, Doris Day, and Natalie Wood, were pleading with him, anxious to get his "Kelly treatment" for themselves. Advertisers wanted him to apply the same "natural glamour" to whatever products they were selling. Howell's roster of clients eventually included Revlon, Dan River, Ford, Helena Rubenstein, and Eastman Kodak.

One client arrived at the studio with an unusual request. The junior senator from Massachusetts, John F. Kennedy, didn't want a finished product; he wanted Howell to photograph him from every angle imaginable. Kennedy took Howell's photos and studied them carefully, learning which were his good angles and which were unflattering. If there was ever a tip-off that the senator had greater political aspirations, this might have been it.

It is possible that JFK's referral to Howell may have come from Grace herself. From their Irish heritage, handsome physicality, and love of sports to their self-made wealth, social prominence, and political aspirations, the Kellys were every inch the Kennedys of Philadelphia. The two clans first met in the late 1940s; just a few months earlier, Jackie Kennedy, then a newlywed, had infiltrated Grace (in a nurse's uniform) into Jack's hospital room to help leaven his spirits as he recuperated from one of his many back surgeries. As a photographer, Howell gave Grace and JFK the same advice: never be photographed looking straight at the camera — he because his eyes were set too close together, she because of her square jaw.

Collier's quickly gave Howell another assignment to photograph Grace. In September of 1955 she began filming *The Swan*, just weeks after *To Catch a Thief* premiered. (Although *Thief* had been shot on the Riviera in spring of 1954, Hitchcock had kept it in the can for more than a year while he readied his TV series, *Alfred Hitchcock Presents*.) *The Swan* was filmed first on MGM sets in Los Angeles, and then on location at the palatial Biltmore estate in North Carolina. In a storyline that foreshadowed future events in her own life, Grace's character, a young princess, marries an older prince from another kingdom.

Many have commented on Grace's seeming aloofness and detachment on the set, and Howell's photos capture the faraway look in her eyes. Her thank-you note to Rainier had become the prelude to a clandestine correspondence with the prince, and their relationship deepened with each exchange of letters. In essence, they fell in love by post. In December, Rainier (traveling as Mr. Grimaldi) arrived for an unofficial visit to Philadelphia, with his physician and Father Tucker, his Irish parish priest, in tow. Tucker had been present at the first meeting in May. After Christmas, with Father Tucker brokering the deal, Rainier asked Jack Kelly for his daughter's hand in marriage. Grace, whose father had vociferously reviled all of her prior boyfriends, finally found a suitor Daddy could approve of. A dowry of $2 million sealed the match.

Trusting Howell completely, Grace invited him to her Fifth Avenue apartment to shoot the first private photos of the radiant couple. Upon meeting Howell for the first time, Rainier is said to have shaken his hand, then torqued it in a playful gesture that was still forceful enough to bring the photographer to his knees. Howell took no offense — they quickly discovered a common interest in scuba diving and underwater photography.

"I don't think I've ever seen a couple more in love," Howell declared. "Every time I turned away to change film or grab another camera, they'd start whispering, holding hands like any just-engaged couple."

Grace eagerly solicited her friend's appraisal of her fiancé. "When I left, Grace walked me to the door," Howell recalled. "'What do you think of him?' she asked. I told her if I were in any position to pass judgment, I'd give my wholehearted approval. Prince or no prince, he's a heck of a nice guy. 'I knew you'd like him, Howell,' she said. 'He's wonderful.'"

Grace returned to Los Angeles to begin shooting *High Society*, the musical remake of *The Philadelphia Story*. Her prince came to visit the set and took a villa in Bel-Air for the duration of his stay. Unhappy with the cheesy prop engagement ring that MGM wanted her to wear for her role as socialite Tracy Lord, Grace asked for permission to wear the 12-carat rock she'd received from Rainier. Not surprisingly, she got it. By virtue of her engagement, Grace had further enhanced her already skyrocketing popularity, and had momentarily gained the upper hand with her studio.

At the end of the shoot, Grace packed up her dressing room and began a round of farewells in Hollywood. She never made another film. "When we married," she later told an interviewer, "my husband said, 'being an actress wasn't a princess-like thing to do.'"

Before Grace departed, Marilyn Monroe is said to have sent a note which read, "So glad you've found a way out of this business." (Monroe herself briefly had been a candidate to become Her Serene Highness, Princess Marilyn, but there was to be no real-life version of *The Prince and the Showgirl*. Even more than her checkered past, Marilyn's inability to pronounce the prince's name — she called him "Prince Reindeer" — put her out of the running.)

MGM gifted Grace with her *High Society* wardrobe, put head costumer Helen Rose in charge of designing her elaborate wedding gown, and let her out of the rest of her contract, which still had several years to run. (Lauren Bacall made the most of what would have been her next role, in *Designing Woman*.) The quid pro quo, however, was that Rainier agreed to permit the studio to film the wedding festivities for a documentary entitled *The Wedding of the Century*. Grace's nuptials were to be an MGM extravaganza.

The wedding was set for April 19, and the media feeding frenzy ramped up as soon as *High Society* wrapped. America had fallen in love with Grace's happily-ever-after fairy tale, and voraciously devoured every detail of her wedding preparations. Grace, who loved being a star but loved her privacy even more, was increasingly upset as the press dogged her footsteps all over Manhattan.

It got worse, then much worse, after she left for Monaco. Grace, her family, and dearest friends commandeered most of the first class cabins on the SS *Constitution* for the eight-day voyage across the Atlantic, but a hundred members of the press were also on board, albeit crammed into less prestigious accommodations. On April 4, Grace set sail into her future from New York's Pier 84, and Howell captured some of her ambivalence about what lay ahead.

With its casinos and its long history as a tax haven, Monaco had been notoriously described by Somerset Maugham as "a sunny place with shady people." The Grimaldis had ruled the country since the 13th century, but there were many skeletons in the family closet, and their domain was tiny. Grace Kelly, A-list movie star, was en route to becoming Her Serene Highness, Princess Grace, wife of the sovereign ruler of a principality that was about as big as the MGM back lot, and just half the size of Central Park.

During the Atlantic crossing, the newshounds were relentless. Grace was obliged to toss them a daily Q&A and photo session to keep them at bay, but they still lurked in odd corners of the ship, hoping to ambush her in an unguarded moment. Fat chance. Grace knew she was fair game any time she was out of her stateroom, and there was only one photographer Grace trusted with her unguarded moments: Howell Conant.

Before the trip, Howell purchased a new 35mm camera, then spent days learning to load and unload it blindfolded, as if it were a service revolver and he was gearing up for battle. Unlike the other photographers, who in his words, "followed each other around" the ship, he was a member of the wedding party — with his cameras stashed in Grace's cabin.

The shipboard media circus was dwarfed by the spectacle that greeted them when they arrived in Monaco. Before Charles and Diana, before Tom and Katie, there was Rainier and Grace — this was truly the first "Wedding of the Century." As a seaplane flew overhead and showered red and white carnations onto the harbor, an armada of small craft raced alongside the *Constitution* as it prepared to rendezvous with Rainier's yacht. Photographers spilled over the gunnels of each boat; more waited onshore, straining for a sight of the princess-to-be. Almost 2,000 members of the press had shoehorned themselves into the tiny princiality. The wedding had mushroomed into a media juggernaut with a momentum all its own.

From that point forward, every facet of the wedding had to be designed to appease, accommodate, or avoid the press. It was a struggle for the royal couple to have any personal time whatsoever, but Howell recorded what little there was. When Grace, clutching her poodle, Oliver, to her bosom, boarded the *Deo Juvante II* to meet up with Rainier, she was escorted by her parents. Everyone else went ashore or stayed behind on the *Constitution* — except Howell.

Howell documented the small civil ceremony on the 8th, but was not in St. Nicholas Cathedral for the wedding the next day. The celebration of the high wedding mass by the Bishop of Monaco was televised in black and white to 30 million people, and of course MGM's cameras were rolling in color for the documentary that Rainier had promised them. The church made what accommodation it could with the cables, lights, sound booms, and cameras that had been placed at key locations within the cathedral.

Prince Rainier covers Howell's head with a light reflector, 1967.

Hundreds of still photographers lined the pews. Grace later told a friend that she had no recollection of the flowers in the sanctuary; all she saw were the exploding flashbulbs of thousands of cameras popping out of the hydrangeas, lilacs, and snapdragons.

Howell's absence from the church was neither a slight nor an oversight. Grace needed him to stay behind in the palace, catching more intimate shots before the ceremony that she would permit no other photographer to get. For his part, Howell needed the extra time to set up his cameras for the reception, and was happy to stay out of the mob scene.

In casting the role of Howell Conant for the movies, the hands-down choice would be Jimmy Stewart — and not just because of his portrayal of L. B. Jeffries, the broken-legged photographer in *Rear Window*. Like Stewart, Howell's homespun humor and mannerisms never strayed far from their Midwestern country-boy roots. He was similarly modest and soft-spoken, but could be direct and to-the-point when necessary. Exuding a quiet competence, Howell was entirely without ego behind the camera. Always a photographer of celebrities, never a "celebrity photographer," the last thing he wanted was to personally overshadow his subject.

He was well aware that his work with Grace and her family had opened the door to a long and lucrative photographic career — with LIFE, among the many other magazines. "Almost everything happened," he said with characteristic modesty, "after I became famous with Grace." Ever grateful, he requited Grace's loyalty to him with loyalty of his own, taking care never to abuse his access. None of his pictures was ever published without her approval — until now. This was not only because of their friendship, but also because there wasn't an ounce of paparazzo in him.

It is Howell Conant who gave us our enduring, memorable images of Grace. Simply put, Grace liked the way she looked when he took her picture, and that was precisely his goal. Whether we conjure up Grace Kelly the movie star, or Princess Grace, Her Serene Highness, it is his likeness of her "natural glamour" that we see in our mind's eye.

Jamaica
On Holiday

Grace had been pleased by Howell's first session with her for *Photoplay* and wanted to give him something to work with for a *Collier's* cover story. She was particularly enamored of the ocean and already knew of Howell's love of scuba, snorkeling, and underwater photography. In a remarkable gesture of trust and confidence, she asked him to join her and her sister Peggy in Jamaica when she took a much-needed holiday after winning her Oscar for *The Country Girl*.

Howell was delighted by Grace's invitation. The relaxed island setting offered him an extraordinary opportunity to shoot casual and candid photographs of Hollywood's leading lady. Playing up her freshness and natural beauty, he was able to reveal the warm, intelligent, and lively woman within. Together, they broke the mold of the traditional movie star "glamour" photograph. It was the beginning of an artistic collaboration that would last the rest of their lives.

Because Grace had taken a dory across Montego Bay, Howell probably liked using such a boat as a prop for this picture.

These shots on the beach are the antithesis of Hollywood bathing beauty photos. Even with the gorgeous scenery of Jamaica in the background, Howell saw that Grace's personality and special magnetism were the focal point of every photograph. On the beach, the playful side of Grace came out as well. One day on the sand, she lightheartedly grabbed him unaware and tossed him over her back with surprising strength.

The photo of Grace emerging from underwater appeared on the cover of the June 24, 1955, issue of *Collier's* and quickly became one of the most acclaimed shots in Hollywood history. More than fifty years later, this iconic image remains fresh, intimate, alluring, and powerful.

Although it appears spontaneous, it was far from effortless. With Howell and Grace both on tiptoes to avoid the spiny sea urchins on the sandy bottom, it took many shots to achieve the precise effect they wanted. Grace posed first with a scuba mask, but Howell knew readers would want to see more of her face. After she removed the mask, it still took eight tries to get it right. Sister Peggy served as the photographer's assistant and held the light reflector; she also shot the photo of Grace and Howell, top left.

What is most special about these Jamaica sessions is Howell's ability to capture the human being behind the movie star. We feel we are seeing the candid, unguarded "everyday" Grace, unassisted by hairdressers or makeup artists. The natural glamour of this 25-year-old woman is both timeless and seductive.

Howell was rarely without his camera when in Grace's presence. And her delighted reactions to his jokes while munching on an orange produce some of the most animated and character-revealing moments we have of this extraordinary woman She's sensual, funny, and strikingly attractive – all at once.

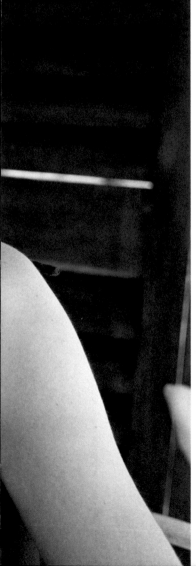

The pictures of Grace reclining on a sofa transcend
the trends and fashion of the time. Eventually we all
but stop seeing both clothing and furniture and focus
on Grace herself. It is her continuing ability to hold us
with her eyes – sometimes playful peek-a-boo, sometimes sultry – that entrances us. Even while she is just
checking her makeup with her sister, she has an aware-
ness of the camera that seems to be reflected in artful
postures.

Shooting with a 35 mm motor-drive (an innovation used primarily by sports photographers at the time) Howell captured these fast-changing images. He said later that he got some good photographic advice from actor James Cagney: to avoid cliché poses, encourage actors to act, shoot the session like a motion picture, and then select the best stills.

"When Grace began playing with the pillow," Howell recalled, "I started shooting. Grace was so myopic she couldn't see ten feet in front her, so she followed the sound of my voice as I directed her. 'Beautiful,' I said over and over again."

Grace had her own way of avoiding Howell's lens.

Howell's own comments on this casual session say it all. "You trusted Grace's beauty; you knew it was not built from clothes and makeup. In New York, Grace would come over to my studio dressed in a sweater, a skirt, and loafers. In Jamaica, she was no different: her hair pulled back, dressed in a simple boy's shirt. This was Grace, natural, unpretentious."

Howell knew how to play up Grace's most powerful feature — her eyes. Framing her face with a large straw hat and obscuring everything below her cheekbones, he leaves us intimately eye-to-eye with one of the most beautiful women in the world. And like Howell, we are mesmerized.

In Jamaica, Howell caught the kaleidoscope that was Grace's multi-faceted personality, and it is apparent that Grace became extremely comfortable working with him in their week together. He was there as she talked with children, surfaced from snorkeling, shopped for a hat, or just stopped to smell the roses, right up to the time she left for home. In the photo top middle, her raised hand was her signal to stop shooting. And he always did. A bond had been formed that would last a lifetime.

Hollywood Studio
The Swan

Two weeks before *The Swan* started filming, *To Catch a Thief* had premiered to both popular and critical acclaim. Coming on the heels of her Best Actress Oscar, Grace was at the pinnacle of her Hollywood fame. Moreover, she was at the top of her art, too. Grace prided herself on professionalism: she knew her lines, knew her blocking, and sometimes knew the camera angles before the director. Watching her in *The Swan* offers an insight into the carefully focused life as an actress that she gave up to be a princess.

Back working on the MGM lot, Grace was supported by Howell, who had another assignment from *Collier's* to document her as she filmed *The Swan*. Since Jamaica, they had not only bonded, but Howell was now Grace's confidant. In the photographs of Grace holding up a card, Howell catches her in the ritual of a studio photographer documenting her hairstyle for matching in future filming sequences.

On the set, Grace was a pro. Howell was fascinated by how seriously she took her job, and how familiar she was with all of the equipment and paraphernalia of a big soundstage. She would often find an offstage vantage point and watch her fellow actors at work. Howell was also impressed by how patient and appreciative she was of the backstage talents essential to moviemaking, especially wardrobe, makeup, and hair. Her hair stylist, Virginia Darcy, was a regular member of Grace's entourage.

Grace enjoyed working with her veteran director, Charles Vidor, who had begun his Hollywood career at the end of the silents. Other than *The Swan*, he is best known for *Cover Girl* (1944) and *Gilda* (1946), both with Rita Hayworth, and *The Joker Is Wild* (1957), with Grace's good friend Frank Sinatra.

Howell often captured Grace in profile, and this photo, right, is a testament to Howell's inventive eye. While shooting pictures of Grace in her dressing room, he noticed a large white lighting panel on the set. He asked Grace to pose in front of it. The backlit portrait is a remarkable combination of soft lighting and a perfect female profile.

Alec Guinness was selected to be Grace's co-star in his first Hollywood film. The two developed a friendship and loved to play practical jokes on each other. For many years, whenever either of them had the opportunity, he or she would slip a tomahawk into the other's bed. Part of the joke was that neither of them would acknowledge it. Above, Vidor is giving some instructions to the two of them before shooting a scene.

Wherever Howell wandered on the set he never took his eyes off Grace.

Although she may have studied fencing at the American Academy of Dramatic Arts, Grace was certainly not a fencer. Nevertheless, she is intently focused on the action and her swordplay is convincing. Her lithe, agile movements show off her form. Her fencing opponent and on-screen love interest, Dr. Nicholas Agi, was played by Gallic heartthrob Louis Jourdan, who was reviewed as "utterly charming."

Howell noticed that Grace could frequently be found knitting, or reading letters, and he would sometimes catch her in solitary moments of deep thought. The letters were from Prince Rainier, but she denied a relationship existed between them. Even to her old friend, Hollywood publicist Rupert Allan, she insisted that there had been no communication between her and the Prince since they met in Monaco.

Howell's eye for candid scenes was remarkable, and Grace's sweet, open candor is apparent in these pictures. He frames some shots of Grace's hair being touched up as though we are eavesdropping on a private moment. In the picture above, she seems to shrug, and faces the lens without artifice.

After two weeks of filming on the MGM lot in Culver City, the production moved to Biltmore House, George Vanderbilt's grand replica of a Loire chateau near Asheville, North Carolina. Director Charles Vidor used its ornate furniture, oversize chandeliers, and sweeping main staircase almost like another character in the film. Although the mansion struck many as a bit over the top (then as now, it was "America's largest home"), Grace seemed to revel in its palatial grandeur even while intently reading (perhaps in French).

As Princess Alexandra in *The Swan*, Grace was revisiting a role she had played in a CBS-TV version in June 1950. She plays a young woman who is tempted to marry a crown prince (Alec Guinness), but falls in love with her brother's tutor (Louis Jourdan), instead. She eventually marries the prince after he tells her that she is like a swan: serene in the water, but more like a goose on the land.

Was Grace trying on a palace for size as she played her scenes at Biltmore House, as some have suggested? However you might see it, there are few women who could sprawl on a grand staircase and look as poised and at ease as she did. She seemed comfortable with the appointments of wealth and grandeur, even as she played a shy, uncertain young woman.

"I don't think Grace even knew I was taking this picture. Here she was in this grand setting, a top star in a major film, yet she was oblivious to all she had, thinking her own thoughts," Howell said. As the other three shots in the series suggest, however, Grace was well aware of the camera and was posing for Howell the entire time.

Although Howell had photographed other movie stars and had been on other movie sets, he apparently had the ability to see *The Swan* through Grace's eyes in a way that he had not seen others. "She remained remote on the set: quiet, pensive," he wrote. "Wrapped in a camel's-hair overcoat, she stood next to this incongruous-looking stage light and I snapped away. For me, this was a new side of Grace, a hardworking actress."

Hollywood Hills Home

Grace came from a wealthy Philadelphia family and kept a New York apartment on Fifth Avenue across from the Metropolitan Museum of Art. Much as she enjoyed the company of many of her fellow actors, New York was always her home. As Howell captured perfectly in some of these photographs, when she was in Hollywood, Grace gave you the feeling that she was "… above it all." Some of these photos date from the early production days of *The Swan*. While she was shooting on the MGM soundstages in Los Angeles, Grace leased a home in the Hollywood Hills from a friend of Greta Garbo, nutritionist Gayelord Hauser.

No doubt Howell was taken by the disparity between the grandiose high-ceilinged white drapes and the simplicity and elegance of the V-cut black dress that Grace was wearing. Not only are the photographs studies in dramatic visual contrasts, but they toy with Grace's "Ice Queen" image. On the following pages, the fur-trimmed dress and demure pose on the settee convey that same "untouchable, above it all" feeling. Posed with her hands on her hips and gazing brazenly into the camera, however, she delivers much more of a dare to the viewer.

Grace's sweet little black poodle, Oliver, was her constant companion. A gift from the Cary Grants, Oliver won her heart instantly.

According to Howell, during the filming of *High Society*, David Niven and his wife offered Grace their Hollywood home so she could meet privately with Prince Rainier, away from the eyes of the press. Howell was invited to one of these gatherings and took some photographs. This is the first time they have been published.

When Grace invited Howell to her New York home to take engagement photographs, he jumped at the prospect. "I hurried over to her Fifth Avenue apartment and saw a Grace Kelly I had never seen before," Howell said. "Jamaica had introduced me to the playful Grace, and *The Swan* to the thoughtful, inward Grace. Now I found standing arm-in-arm with Prince Rainier of Monaco, Grace Kelly Number Three, a woman in love."

Voyage to Monaco

Howell captured the mob of photographers clustered on New York's Pier 84 as the *Constitution* set sail on April 4, 1956. One reporter wryly said the scene was "just like a Hollywood version of a boat departing." Despite all the journalists left behind, a hundred more made the crossing with Grace and paid first-class fare for the privilege of bunking three or four to a room.

Once Grace had waved farewell to the fog-shrouded Statue of Liberty, she returned to her stateroom to find a wedding present from "Philip of Magnesia." When she saw that the box contained a new leash for Oliver, she immediately realized who the giver was. Alfred Hitchcock, who had turned down an invitation to attend the wedding, had sent a gift from his dog instead.

Grace had hoped that her impending marriage would diminish the attentions of the paparazzi and the endless magazine intrusions into her life, but she was greatly mistaken. Edmund Duffy, the dean of New York's shipping news reporters, described her departure as "the biggest shipside news conference in thirty years." The main event was already being called "The Wedding of the Century." It would be the most reported social event of that publicity-conscious decade, televised live to 30 million viewers.

Grace's private thoughts were less celebratory. "The day we left, our ship was surrounded by fog, and that's the way I felt, as if I were sailing off into the unknown," she later said. "I couldn't help wondering, 'What's going to happen to me? What will this new life be like?'"

NO ADMITTANCE
TO BRIDGE
EXCEPT ON BUSINESS

As they crossed the Atlantic on the SS *Constitution*, no one except Grace knew that Howell was on assignment for LIFE. Their friendship gave him unique access to her movements on the ship; thus he alone was able to catch the private moment when Grace walked her dogs on the deck each morning. It was always a given that her beloved poodle Oliver would accompany her to Monaco. At the start of the journey, he was joined by a not entirely housebroken Weimaraner, a bon voyage gift from old Philadelphia friends.

In her trademark sunglasses and multi-megawatt smile, Grace obliges a family member by posing at the rail for a snapshot. At right, she relaxes in a small private section of the deck.

The Kelly party numbered about seventy, including her parents, Jack and Margaret, and her sister Peggy (her matron of honor), three of her bridesmaids — Judy Kanter, Maree Frisby, and Bettina Thompson — and more than fifty friends. The celebratory feeling of the wedding party made the voyage one long festivity, or as it was described by a bridesmaid, "a floating summer camp." Jack Kelly paid the tab for everyone in the group.

To satisfy the photographers' demands for images of Grace, Howell and MGM publicist Morgan Hudgins conspired to arrange a daily photo op. The shuffleboard scene with some children was one such event. In exchange, the photographers pledged to leave her in peace, but that accord was quickly breached. Paparazzi lurked all over the ship in hope of a "Grace sighting." Howell caught a scene of her hiding behind a newspaper after one photographer had spotted her through the window.

Although Grace made appearances at the evening dinners and parties on board (and, of course, the obligatory lifeboat drill on the first day at sea), she spent a great deal of time in her cabin, either eating a solitary meal, writing letters, or handling a large stack of paperwork.

During the eight days at sea, every dinner was a special occasion, with men in tuxedos and ladies in evening dresses. There were endless rounds of toasts, lengthy speeches expounding on the greatness of the Kelly family, and silly party hats. The bride's father, Jack Kelly, happily paid for these extravaganzas because Rainier – and MGM – had relieved him of the traditional father's obligation to pay for the wedding. Grace herself ducked in and out of the evening events, preferring smaller, more low-key gatherings.

Observers suggested that Grace was tying up all of her loose ends in preparation for her new life, but one shipboard pastime she never missed was charades. As a bright actress with wonderful control of gestures and facial expressions, it was a parlor game at which she excelled. On charade nights, Howell set up in the ship's Tattoo Room, where the Kelly entourage gathered after dinner. In keeping with their competitive nature, there was nothing easy about the phrases players had to act out. In the sequence on the next two pages, Grace is dramatizing "watch the danger line," and ends with a sensational bow that Howell manages to capture beautifully from above. On this page, she delights in figuring out "heat transfer and thermodynamics" from the gyrations of agent Jay Kanter.

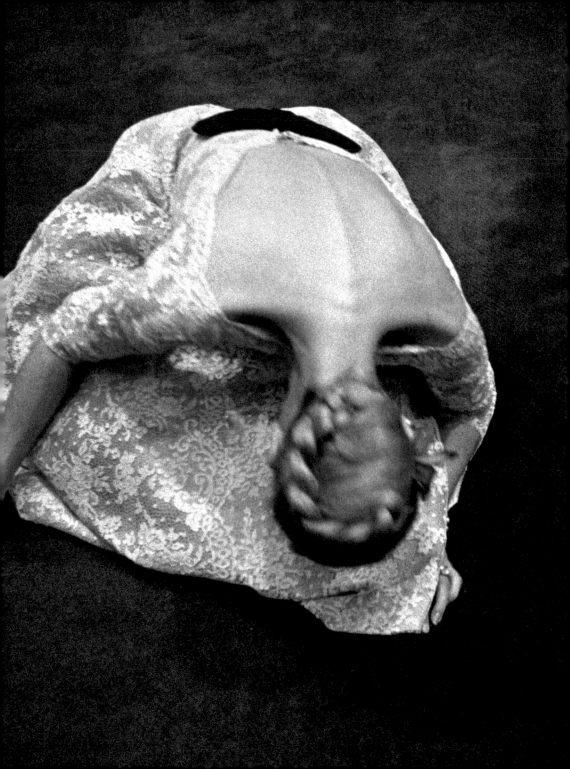

Monaco

At 10 a.m. on April 12, 1956, the USS *Constitution* arrived at the mouth of Monaco's small harbor. Most of the 23,000 residents of the principality waved from balconies and rooftops to greet the *Constitution*. They were joined by an estimated 2,000 reporters and photographers from all over the world. The cleverest of the journalists had commandeered speedboats and other small craft – anything afloat – in the hope of getting closer to the action. Because the *Constitution* was too large to dock in the yacht basin, His Serene Highness, Prince Rainier III, came out on his yacht, the *Deo Juvante II*, to greet his bride.

Grace looked lovely in an elegant navy blue silk coat and a large white organza clamshell chapeau. The hat was a sensible substitute for a veil, and it also shaded her eyes. The press complained that the hat obscured her features, but on this important day Grace had not selected her head covering with them in mind. It was Howell's photographs that benefited most from her choice. Like a photographer's white umbrella, the sheer hat diffused the light, softening any harsh shadows from the sun. Moreover, it gave Howell an ideal frame for her face. After Grace walked down the gangplank to the *Deo Juvante II*, Rainier welcomed his bride-to-be with nothing more than a restrained handshake. The prince had a lifelong aversion to displaying any sort of affection in public.

Escorted into the royal courtyard of the palace, Grace and her mother follow Monsignor Gilles Barthe, Bishop of Monaco, who would perform the wedding ceremony, and Father Francis Tucker, who Rainier often referred to as their cupid. Note that a much decorated royal chamberlain stands at attention nearby, holding a beribboned Oliver by his new leash. The horseshoe-shaped royal courtyard staircase is a stunning white marble entrance to the Galerie d'Hercule, which runs parallel to the state apartments.

The Royal Wedding

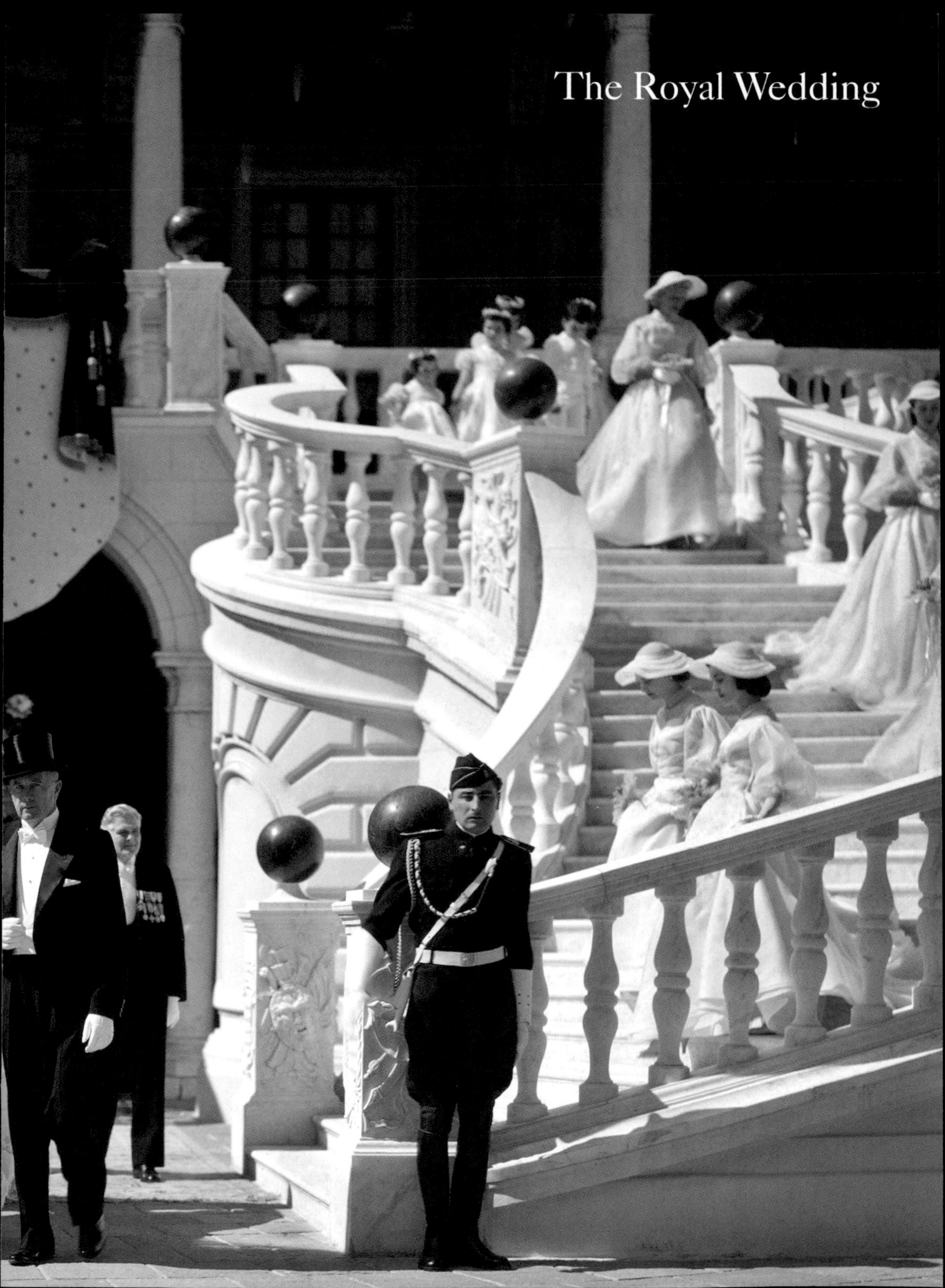

On April 18, 1956, Grace and Rainier were married in a civil ceremony before a small group of eighty guests. Grace wore a rose pink taffeta dress covered in Alençon lace designed by MGM's Helen Rose, white gloves, and a Juliet cap. Rainier wore a handsome morning coat with grey tie and striped trousers.

Following the civil ceremony in the throne room, Howell caught the happy smiles of both Rainier and Grace at the elegant luncheon. Later that day, they hosted an immense garden party on the grounds of the palace, where 3,000 Monégasques crowded in to toast their prince and his bride.

"The Wedding of the Century" at St. Nicholas Cathedral the next day was a high mass with 600 people in attendance, including Aristotle Onassis, Cary Grant, Aga Khan, King Farouk, Ava Gardner, Randolph Churchill, David Niven, Gloria Swanson and Somerset Maugham.

That night, the royal couple joined the citizens of Monaco at a gala celebration in the Opera House. Later, no doubt near exhaustion, they waved to more crowds of admirers and well-wishers from a window of the palace.

Howell posed the bridesmaids, flower girls, and a tranquil Grace just as they were to leave for St. Nicholas Cathedral. Grace's bridesmaids were her oldest friends: Judy Kanter, Maree Frisby, Bettina Thompson, Carolyn Scott, Sally Parrish, and Rita Gam. Along with the matron of honor, Grace's sister Peggy, they wore yellow organza dresses (a gift from Neiman Marcus). The flower girls were dressed in white. Grace found her friends' presence comforting, but the event was overwhelming.

A veiled Grace adjusts Carolyn Scott's picture hat. Always attuned to details, she wanted her bridesmaids to look perfect.

Grace's wedding dress was the crowning achievement of Helen Rose's career, and the most expensive garment she ever designed. The dress, valued at more than $7,200 at the time, had been worked on feverishly in top secret for six weeks by a platoon of three dozen seamstresses. Suitably feminine and elegant, it was an ivory high-necked, long-sleeved gown with a fitted bodice with an overlay of 125-year-old rose point lace. The cut of the gown accentu-ated Grace's tiny waist; its voluminous bell skirt of silk taffeta, peau de soie, tulle, and lace billowed with hundreds of yards of fabric. The circular veil added ninety more yards of tulle, highlighted with seed pearls and affixed to a small fitted headpiece. After the ceremony, Grace donated her gown to the Phila-delphia Museum of Art. In the summer of 2007 it was loaned to Monaco for a retrospective at the Grimaldi Forum on the 25th anniversary of her death.

The religious ceremony took place on April 19, 1956, in St. Nicholas Cathedral. Grace asked Howell to forego shooting in the church so he could set up for these formal photographs after the wedding. The bridal party and the family group are elegantly dressed, and Rainier and Grace make a stunning couple — she in a wedding dress designed by Helen Rose, and he in a military uniform of his own design. Rainier had earned his medals for valor as an artillery officer in World War II. They included the Croix de Guerre and an appointment as a chevalier in the Legion of Honor.

A champagne buffet in the palace courtyard followed the high mass at the cathedral. At the end of the meal, Rainier sliced the newlywed's six-tier wedding cake with his sword. Once again, Howell had exclusive access for up-close-and-personal photographs of the royal couple at the reception, even capturing the rather tired bride as she smiled at her new husband.

Howell had the great photographer's instinct to be there at perhaps the most intimate moment of the lengthy wedding ceremonies. Their grins of joy are, of course, happiness at having the moment to walk in the palace gardens, high above Monaco, and – for a moment – relax. It is touching to note that one of the lasting memorials to Princess Grace is a rose garden named after her on the slope of Monaco's Fontvieille Park, with some 4,000 rose bushes.

The newlyweds left the palace to receive one last wedding present, a cream and black Rolls Royce that was a gift from the people of Monaco. Grace changed into her going away clothes and, after a farewell spin through the streets of the principality, the couple headed to the harbor to begin their honeymoon. Howell was already standing on the deck of the *Deo Juvante II* when they boarded, Grace with her trademark camel-hair coat over her arm, to embark on their Mediterranean honeymoon cruise and their new life together.

Grace: The Princess Years

appily, the remarkable collaboration between Grace and Howell continued for a quarter century after the wedding. During those years, Howell would visit Monaco once or twice a year, always with the ostensible purpose of a magazine assignment, but usually returning with those magical pictures that give us insights into Grace's moods and personality as she grew into her new life as wife, mother, and royal role model.

Nine months after the wedding, Grace invited Howell back to Monaco as she prepared to give birth to her first child. He took pictures of Princess Caroline when she was just hours old, and returned for her christening forty days later. It was a scenario repeated with the arrival of each royal offspring. Howell was on hand for the birth of Prince Albert in March of 1958, and of Princess Stéphanie in February of 1965. Thereafter, he was invited almost annually to take an "official" portrait of Grace and her family, and to provide an updated Christmas card picture of the family for friends and citizens of Monaco. In each instance, he used his remarkable access to capture touching family moments that never could have been planned or posed.

Grace took on her duties as a princess with the same thoroughness and dedication she had given to her Hollywood career. She established the Princess Grace Foundation to support local artists and craftsmen, and brought in noted Russian ballet mistress Marika Besobrasova to open the Academie de Danse Classique Princesse Grace, where Caroline studied. Grace was one of the first celebrities to speak out in support of breastfeeding, and was president of the La Leche League of Monaco. In 1968, she furthered her love of flowers by starting the Monaco Garden Club. In all, however, her favorite charity activity was probably Monaco's orphanage. She visited the children there regularly, and took considerable interest in their education. Each year, she personally selected a Christmas gift for every child.

Although these charitable efforts were rewarding, Grace's artistic collaboration with Howell became her primary outlet for creative self-expression in her years as a princess. Reading aloud and playacting with her children could never have been adequate for an Academy Award winning actress. Although she fulfilled her role as a royal leader of Monaco, she missed acting greatly. Grace had always held on to the hope that she could eventually resume her Hollywood career, but it was not until 1962, when she was forced to turn down Alfred Hitchcock's offer of the lead in *Marnie*, that she knew that door had closed forever.

Rainier, it turned out, was not the problem. Her costar would have been Sean Connery, red hot in his prime as James Bond. Although the prince had given his approval, he was overruled by his constituents. "The reaction came in," recalled actress and bridesmaid Rita Gam, "from 3,500 Monégasques who refused to see her being kissed onscreen."

Fashion became yet another outlet for Grace's theatrical talents. She favored designs that were at the same time simple, classic, and patrician, and she worked with the best haute couture houses, including Christian Dior, Balenciaga, Givenchy, Lanvin, and Yves Saint Laurent. Princess Grace became a fashion icon, and her glamour and style transformed Monaco into a contemporary port-of-call for high society. Fifty years later, the Kelly bag remains a fashion classic.

Howell continued to be among the closest friends of both Grace and Rainier right up to her tragic death. Princess Grace died of injuries sustained behind the wheel of her Rover 3500 when it plunged off a cliff on a twisty stretch of the Moyenne Corniche, not far from Roc Agel, the family retreat. Princess Stéphanie was in the car with her mother, but escaped with minor injuries. Although brake failure was initially suspected, it was later confirmed that Princess Grace had suffered a stroke.

It is a tribute to the respect Grace commanded during her years as a princess that European royalty attended her funeral in great numbers. Howell Conant was also there — the first time and only time he traveled to Monaco without his cameras. He continued to correspond with Rainier, and always consulted with him regarding the publication of his pictures of Grace. For the remaining twenty years of his life, Howell found it difficult to speak about Grace, and whenever he did, there was a catch in his voice, and often a tear.

Her Serene Highness
Princess Grace

"As an actress, I'd always thought I wanted to play a wide assortment of parts," Grace said, "but in life, once I agreed to be a princess, I was typecast." Grace was everyone's idea of what a princess should be. Beloved by the citizens of Monaco, she seemed to handle the formal occasions and the royal trappings with remarkable ease. Intuitively regal, never imperious, her bearing and the clothing she selected for her various roles enhanced her already elevated status as a worldwide fashion icon.

When she became a princess, life changed in unexpected ways for Grace. What didn't change was her collaboration with Howell Conant. He continued to document her transformation from actress to princess. He captured Grace's joy in motherhood and was there as she visited an orphanage, wrapped Christmas presents, or went sailing.

Scenes from a Marriage

Nine months and four days after her wedding, Grace gave birth to Princess Caroline Louise Marguerite. A year later, on March 14, 1958, Prince Albert Alexandre Louis Pierre, the present ruler of Monaco, arrived. The family was completed when Princess Stéphanie Marie Elisabeth made an appearance on February 1, 1965. Perhaps in reaction to his own unhappy childhood, Rainier went along with Grace's firmly held notions of a child-centered household, and the Grimaldi children were raised in close contact with their parents.

Shortly before they were married, Prince Rainier bestowed on Grace the sash of the Order of St. Charles, Monaco's highest honor. Grace wore it on almost every formal occasion. In this official portrait, she looks every inch a regal presence. For these formal photographs, Rainier almost always dressed in the military uniform of the Napoleonic era.

For the first time since their honeymoon, the couple ventured publicly out of Monaco around the time of their tenth wedding anniversary, right. In Seville, Grace was crowned queen of a folk festival, and she dressed appropriately for the occasion, wearing a beautiful lace mantilla. Unfortunately, the pleasure of the trip was marred by constant intrusions by paparazzi, who followed the couple.

In 1959, Howell accompanied the royal family on a vacation in the Swiss Alps. With baby Caroline in tow, they rented a chalet in Schonried, near Gstaad. Howell could never pronounce the name of the nearby town and Grace would correct him, laughing: "Shtad, Howell! Shtad! You don't pronounce the 'g'!" Howell's photos revealed the playful mood of the royal couple, as Rainier, sporting a beard, teases Grace while she vamps in one of his hats. Howell was also there for many warm scenes of family life in the palace.

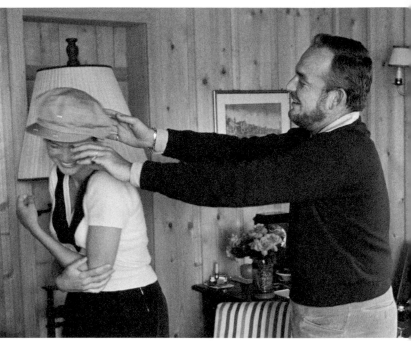

Princess Grace was a very attentive mother with all of her children. The lovely photograph of Princess Grace reading to them with the now greying Oliver lying at her feet is typical of her delight in reading out loud. The children got the benefit of her acting skills and loved stories such as *Alice in Wonderland*, which Grace read either in English or her now perfect French. They joined her when she reviewed the parading troops. Howell noted, "I loved photographing Grace when she was with her children, if only because she could get so involved with them that she paid little attention to me and my camera. At the moment when I snapped this photo [the one of Princess Grace and Caroline by the piano, left], nothing was more important than fixing Caroline's curls." Rainier was also an attentive and active father.

As the years passed, more of Howell's photographic images of Grace and her family were serious and formal, partially because each year he would come to Monaco to shoot the family Christmas card. During these visits, he found Grace periodically playing with her children or climbing aboard one of the royal yachts, but the pictures increasingly became carefully posed images of royalty for public consumption. Although he never lost his knack for catching Grace in lighter moods, giddily bouncing on a trampoline or clowning with giant sunglasses, there was no question that she had added another layer of dignity to her public persona. She had become Monaco's proper princess.

Howell's pictures of Grace aging continued to hold our attention. In private, the royal couple enjoyed informality in both dress and behavior, and Howell caught both with his cameras. The picture of Grace and Rainier alone together in 1980, leaning on a fence at Roc Agel, their family retreat, is a telling portrait. They appear relaxed and at ease with one another, a couple that has survived the rough spots of life to reach a quiet contentment in their relationship. As with his famous photo in the water in Jamaica, however, Howell also caught something extra. Though dignified, as a princess ought to be, Grace retains her inner sparkle, and she again invites us to speculate on whatever turmoils or secret thoughts lie behind that Mona Lisa smile.

"For me, this picture personifies Princess Grace," Howell had said, "as the shot from Jamaica, of her head rising from the water, personifies Grace Kelly, the actress."